Growing up Safe

Safety
at the pool

Illustrated by Sue Wilkinson

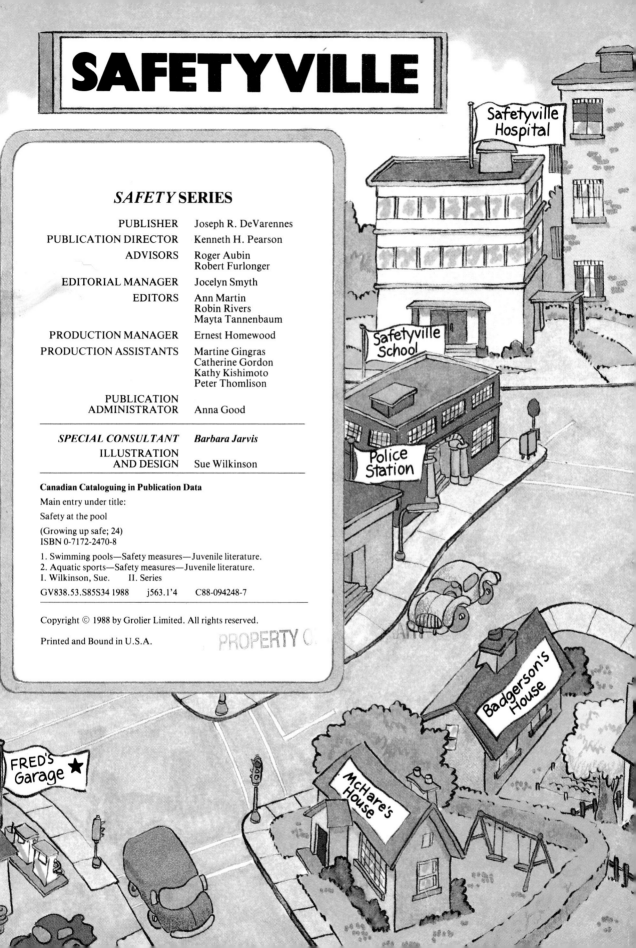

SAFETYVILLE

SAFETY SERIES

PUBLISHER	Joseph R. DeVarennes
PUBLICATION DIRECTOR	Kenneth H. Pearson
ADVISORS	Roger Aubin
	Robert Furlonger
EDITORIAL MANAGER	Jocelyn Smyth
EDITORS	Ann Martin
	Robin Rivers
	Mayta Tannenbaum
PRODUCTION MANAGER	Ernest Homewood
PRODUCTION ASSISTANTS	Martine Gingras
	Catherine Gordon
	Kathy Kishimoto
	Peter Thomlison
PUBLICATION ADMINISTRATOR	Anna Good

SPECIAL CONSULTANT	*Barbara Jarvis*
ILLUSTRATION AND DESIGN	Sue Wilkinson

Canadian Cataloguing in Publication Data

Main entry under title:

Safety at the pool

(Growing up safe; 24)
ISBN 0-7172-2470-8

1. Swimming pools—Safety measures—Juvenile literature.
2. Aquatic sports—Safety measures—Juvenile literature.
I. Wilkinson, Sue.   II. Series

GV838.53.S85S34 1988   j563.1'4   C88-094248-7

Badgerson Family

Dad Mom Kim Timmy Tina

Come join Kim, Timmy and Tina Badgerson as they find out everything they need to know about pool safety.

DO NOT RELY ON INFLATABLE TOYS TO SUPPORT YOU. LEARN TO SWIM.

ALWAYS SWIM WITH A GROWNUP.

DO NOT RUN ON THE POOL DECK. YOU MIGHT SLIP AND FALL.

STAY IN THE SHALLOW END UNTIL YOU CAN SWIM WELL.

BE CAREFUL WHEN JUMPING OR DIVING INTO A POOL. MAKE SURE THAT YOU WON'T LAND ON ANYONE.

NEVER DIVE INTO THE SHALLOW END.

3.5 m

LIFE-SAVING EQUIPMENT IS FOR EMERGENCIES. DO NOT PLAY WITH IT.

NO PUSHING IN OR NEAR A POOL.

DO NOT TAKE GLASS THINGS IN OR NEAR A POOL.

IT IS NOT SAFE TO TAKE
ANYTHING ELECTRICAL NEAR
WATER.

NEVER PLAY ON A POOL COVER.

ONLY GO INTO A PRIVATE SWIMMING POOL IF YOU ARE INVITED TO DO SO.

YOU CAN SWIM SAFELY ONE
HOUR AFTER A MEAL.